by

James Brady

How to Be a Detective
by James Brady

Copyright © 2024

All Rights reserved.

No part of this publication may be reproduced, stored in a retrieval system, or transmitted in any form or by any means, electronic, mechanical, photocopying or Otherwise, without the written permission of the publisher.
The author/editor asserts the moral right to be identified as the author/editor of this work.

ISBN: 978-93-62209-65-8

Published by

DOUBLE 9 BOOKS

2/13-B, Ansari Road
Daryaganj, New Delhi – 110002
info@double9books.com
www.double9books.com
Tel. 011-40042856

This book is under public domain

ABOUT THE AUTHOR

James Brady, renowned for his insightful and engaging writing, unveils a captivating masterpiece in "How to Be a Detective." With meticulous detail and expert guidance, Brady demystifies the art of detection, offering readers a comprehensive manual for honing their investigative skills. From unraveling complex mysteries to mastering the subtle nuances of interrogation, Brady's expertise shines through in every chapter. Through clear prose and practical advice, he equips readers with the tools and techniques necessary to navigate the intricate world of sleuthing with confidence and precision. Whether delving into the psychology of criminals or deciphering clues left behind at the scene of a crime, Brady's book serves as an indispensable companion for aspiring detectives and seasoned investigators alike. With a keen understanding of human nature and a knack for unraveling the most perplexing cases, Brady's "How to Be a Detective" stands as a testament to his mastery of the genre. Imbued with suspense, intrigue, and invaluable insights, this seminal work cements Brady's legacy as a foremost authority on the art of detection.

CONTENTS

INTRODUCTORY
　　OLD KING BRADY TELLS WHY HE WROTE THE BOOK 7

CHAPTER I
　　A LETTER FROM DETECTIVE KEAN 10

CHAPTER II
　　CAUGHT BY A HAT 24

CHAPTER III
　　SHADOWING 36

CHAPTER IV
　　DISGUISES 51

CHAPTER V
　　RINGING IN 63

INTRODUCTORY
OLD KING BRADY TELLS WHY HE WROTE THE BOOK

Some of my friends will no doubt wonder why I should leave the beaten track and contrary to the course I have always adopted of furnishing notes to my friend, the New York detective, write a book myself.

The fact of the matter is the number of boys who love to read my adventures has grown to be so numerous—it is away up in the hundreds of thousands Mr. Tousey tells me—that their wishes have got to be respected.

For several years they have been asking for instructions from me which will transform them from school-boys into full-fledged detectives, as though touched by a magician's wand.

The idea of such a thing!

But there are many who would like to become detectives if they could, and are willing to take time to learn the business, which, believe me, has to be learned like everything else.

Of course there may be some "smart Alecks" who have picked up the business—doubtless there are—but like extra smart people in other lines they do not often make it a success.

Therefore I say that to give a series of rules which, if followed, will make a boy a detective, would only be to make a fool of myself and my pupils too.

It can't be done.

In our business no two situations are ever alike; the case you are working on to-day is totally different from the case of to-morrow, and the case of next week different again from either, and so it goes.

What I propose to do, therefore, is to tell how I made one boy—no, two—detectives. Let their experiences serve for others to go by.

First, however, let me give a list of the particular qualities and attainments necessary to make a good detective, and say also a few words on the different kinds of detectives—the good and the bad.

QUALIFICATIONS OF A GOOD DETECTIVE

1. Indomitable courage and good health.

2. Strict honesty.

3. A fair education. *Necessary.*

4. A knowledge of languages. *Highly desirable.*

5. The ability to read men readily. (This is a quality which will improve by practice. It cannot be expected at first.)

6. Perseverance.

7. An agreeable disposition; the ability to make one's self popular among men.

8. An acquaintance with the methods of changing the facial appearance and arranging disguises. (This is perhaps the hardest thing of all to acquire. Most detectives will not disclose these secrets. The help of a good theatrical costumer, or an actor should be sought. Practice makes perfect—don't forget that.)

9. Capability of careful thought and the ability to weigh evidence, and not to allow yourself to be deceived by appearances.

10. Caution.

11. Control of the temper.

12. Last, and most important of all, Common Sense.

Now I say that unless a boy possesses to a certain degree these twelve qualifications he better not think about becoming a detective.

The office is an important one and performs a great use in the world, but it can easily be prevented and the detective degraded to the level of a hired spy.

Never in my life have I undertaken a case where I have not at least *believed* that I was working on the right side.

I don't propose to sell my services to bad men to work out bad ends.

Others are not so particular. Such are not true detectives—they are simply spies.

As to the means of getting the opportunity to learn the business of detective, I can only say that it is just like everything else; there are all sorts of ways.

Application to some good private detective agency will give you that information. If it is not convenient to do that, consult some honest detective, either police or private, and he may be able to tell you how to get a start.

For a boy to throw up his business and go a stranger to any of our great cities with the idea of at once blooming out into a detective can only bring disappointment.

You have got to start right to come out right.

There are hundreds of detectives, moreover, who barely make a living. Only the experienced and the skillful grow rich, for it is in this business precisely the same as in everything else.

Only hard work, patience, pluck and perseverance will win the fight.

I remain, my dear readers,
Your obedient servant,
James Brady.

New York, April 1, 1890.

CHAPTER I
A LETTER FROM DETECTIVE KEAN

One of the brightest and most successful of our New York detectives is Mr. Samuel Kean, at present attached to Pinkerton's Agency.

He was one of my pupils, and a better one I never had.

I have therefore selected a few of his early cases to illustrate the kind of work that a young detective has to engage in.

Let him tell about his first case himself. I thought it would be more interesting to let him do his own talking, and accordingly wrote him and asked that he would describe his first case in his own way. Here is the answer I received:

New York, March 20th, 1890.

> My Dear Mr. Brady,—You ask me to write you a letter and tell you all about my first case and how I became a detective.
>
> Now it will be very easy for me to do this, for I have never forgotten a single thing that happened that night, and I don't believe I ever shall forget, if I live to be a hundred years old; and yet, after all, it wasn't much of a case. It would have been mere child's play to you if you had been in my position, which, of course, you wouldn't. For you wouldn't have allowed yourself to be deceived the way I was—that's one thing sure.
>
> I was between eighteen and nineteen then, and had left school some six months before I got the idea of being a detective.
>
> My father was dead against it from the start, and my mother wouldn't let me even mention the subject, but you see I had been reading about you and your wonderful cases in the New York Detective Library, and I got an idea that I would like no better fun than to be a detective myself.

"Pooh! You haven't got the courage to be a detective!" exclaimed my father one evening, when I broached the subject for the hundredth time. "You'd run at the first fire, Sam."

"Did I get my cowardice from you, sir?" I asked mildly.

"Not much! You got it from — —"

"Don't say it came from my side of the house, Mr. Kean!" snapped my mother. "My father was all through the Mexican war, and you got a substitute when they drafted you time of the Southern rebellion. The boy is a plaguey sight braver than you are."

Now I had my mother on my side from that moment.

The result of my father's fling was a big family row, which ended in the old gentleman's getting me a letter of introduction to you, Mr. Brady. I took the letter down to your office one morning, and that's the way it began.

"I don't know about this," was the first thing you said. "Young men born with silver spoons in their mouths rarely make good detectives. Don't you think you'd better try your hand at some other line of business, my friend?"

I told you that I meant to be a detective if I died for it, I believe, or something of that sort. I know I wanted very much to speak with you alone, and felt rather mad because there was another person in the office, a slim, freckled-faced, red-headed young chap of about my own age, whose cheap dress showed that he belonged to the working classes. I had rather a contempt for him, and was just wishing he'd get out, when you sent him out without my asking.

"Now that fellow has got the very kind of stuff in him that good detectives are made of," you remarked, and I remember I inwardly laughed at you.

"Why, he's nothing but an ordinary street boy," I thought to myself. You know who I refer to—Dave Doyle.

Then you talked to me a long time, and asked me all about my education and my health, besides a whole lot of other questions, which at the time seemed to me were of no account, but which I now understand to be most important.

As almost every answer I gave seemed to be the very one you did not want, I had just about made up my mind that you were going to reject me entirely, when all at once you surprised me by saying that I could try it if I wanted to for two months, after which you would either pay me something regular in the way of wages, or tell me to get out.

I don't suppose you know it, Mr. Brady, but when I left your office that morning I felt about nine feet high.

I was sure of success, and I firmly believe that it was the very certainty I felt that made me succeed.

I was to report next day, and I did so.

You put me in charge of a man named Mulligan, one of the lowest type of police detectives, who was looking for a pickpocket called Funeral Pete, a fellow who made a point of robbing people at funerals.

"Funeral Pete" had taken alarm, and was in hiding, and Mulligan and I undertook to find out where.

Well, we didn't find out, but I learned a lot of other things, for Mulligan dragged me through nearly every dive in New York.

I was amazed and not a little startled.

Had I got to mix up with such dreadful people as these in order to make myself a detective?

It made me sick to think of it, still I had no notion of turning back.

This state of affairs kept up for a couple of weeks.

First I was sent out with one detective, then with another. There was no disguising, no shadowing, nor shooting. Everything seemed terribly commonplace.

One night I spoke to you about my disappointment. I told you this wasn't the sort of thing I wanted, that I had expected to go about disguised with wigs and false mustaches, carrying revolvers, bowie-knives, dark lanterns and handcuffs in my pockets, and all that sort of thing.

How you laughed! I shall never forget it.

"Why, bless you, some one's got to do the kind of work you're doing," you said, "and very often just such work becomes necessary in the most important cases. However, if you're tired of it I'll try you on another sort of a job and see how you make out."

You took me into the office and began to talk.

"Did you ever study bookkeeping?" you asked.

"Yes," said I.

"How good a bookkeeper are you?"

"I can do double entry."

"As they teach it in schools?"

"Yes."

"Humph. I'm afraid that won't amount to much, still, you can try."

"Try what?"

"Listen to me! To-morrow morning you go down to No. —— Broadway, office of the Eagle Steamship Line, and say I'm the bookkeeper Old King Brady spoke of. That will be enough. They'll engage you."

"What for?"

"To keep books, of course."

"But I don't want to be a book-keeper—I want to be a detective."

"Hold on, hold on! A detective has got to be anything and everything. You will take the job and go to work. You will also keep your eyes open and try and find out who is robbing the safe every night or two, of small amounts—do you understand?"

"Ah! I'm going to be put on a case at last then?"

"Of course you are. There is no information to give you except that some one of your fellow employees is a thief, and I want to catch him. You must watch every man in the office and you mustn't let one of them know that you are watching. As for further instructions, I haven't got any to give. It is a case for you to show what you are made of. I will give you one week to accomplish something in. If you have nothing to report at the end of that time, I shall put on another man."

Wasn't that putting me on my mettle?

Well, I thought so then, and I haven't changed my opinion since.

I resolved to show you what sort of stuff I was made of before the week had passed.

Of course, when I presented myself at the Eagle steamship office I was engaged at once.

The line ran down to South America somewhere—Brazil, if I remember rightly—and the proprietor's name was Sandman, a bald-headed, snuffy old Scotchman who was terribly exercised about the robberies, but I felt very sure, from what I heard the other clerks say, that, even if I did succeed in catching the thief, I needn't look for any big reward, for, with one voice, they pronounced Mr. Sandman "meaner than mud."

Now the store occupied by Mr. Sandman was on the west side of Broadway and had a half-story opening on a level with the New Church street sidewalk in the rear, where the freight was kept and from which most of the shipping was done.

The clerks all had desks inside a big wire partition down near the door, and old man Sandman's office was in the rear, while the safe which was being robbed stood between the last desk and the private office, with only the door leading down into the freight department between.

I was immediately put to work on the outward freight book.

It was simple enough. I hadn't the least trouble in keeping the book, but how to worm myself into the secrets of my fellow clerks—there was the rub.

There were six of them altogether.

Jim Gleason, the "inward freight," on my left; old Mr. Buzby, the head book-keeper, on my right; Hen Spencer, the foreign correspondent, stood nearest the safe all day, and then there was a fellow named Mann, another named Grady, and an office boy; besides these, there were the fellows in the freight department down-stairs.

Which out of all this crowd was the thief?

Never did I so fully realize my want of experience in the business as when I had been in the office of the Eagle Line a few days, without being able to accomplish anything more than to get every one down on me.

"He's always snoopin' about and listenin' to what a feller says," I overheard Grady say to Mr. Buzby one day.

"That's so," replied the book-keeper. "I seen him peekin' into the safe the other day. I don't see what old Sandman wants him for anyhow. He's slower than death about his work and as thick-headed as a mule."

I was in the closet blacking my boots at the time for it was near the hour to close.

Oh, how mad I was! for I knew they were talking about me.

I made up my mind then and there that old Buzby was the thief. "Anyway," I reasoned when I left, soon after, "if it ain't him, who is it? He's the only one besides Mr. Sandman who has the key."

Such was my theory at the end of the first week.

I pumped Jim Gleason next to me, the pleasantest fellow in the whole office, a little inclined to be fast, perhaps, if his everlasting chatter about girls, policy and horse races meant anything, but so kind, and seemed to take such a fancy to me, that I couldn't help liking him better than any one else in the crowd for all that.

From him I learned that the robberies had been going on for a long time, even continued since I came there. This greatly surprised me. The safe was an old one, he said, and Sandman was too mean to buy a better. Somebody who had a key was doing the stealing, Gleason thought, and he openly hinted that Mr. Buzby was the thief.

Saturday night came, and according to orders I went up to your office to report.

"How are you getting on?" says you.

"Not at all," says I, "except that I'm certain that old Buzby, the book-keeper, is doing the stealing."

"Can you prove it?"

"Oh, no!"

"What makes you think so?"

"The clerks all think so."

"When you say all which ones do you really mean?"

"Jim Gleason for one—Spencer for another."

"Which one told you this?"

"Gleason."

"How came he to tell you?"

"Well, he works next to me, and we got to talking."

"Did you tell him you were a detective?" you asked, turning on me suddenly.

"Well, I'm afraid he guesses it," I replied, turning red.

"Why?"

"From something he said."

"After you had given yourself away?"

I grew redder still.

"I was asking him about the robbery, and he suddenly asked me what I wanted to know so much about it for."

"And what did you say?"

"I said, 'of nothing, just curiosity;' then he asked me how much they paid me, and told me in a whisper that he'd caught on to my little racket, and knew I was a detective."

"And you denied it?"

"Yes."

"Be very sure he didn't believe you," you said. Then you told me that I was a fool to give myself away, and I expected to hear you say "don't go there again. I'll put another man on," but you didn't, and Monday morning I went back to the desk the same as usual. I had no instructions from you how to act, for we had been interrupted in our conversation, and I hadn't seen you since.

Monday night Jim Gleason asked me out to have a drink, and I went and took a beer with him. While we were in the saloon Hen Spencer dropped in.

"So there's another new man taken on," he remarked.

"Who?" asked Gleason.

"Feller in the freight room down-stairs. Wouldn't wonder if he was a detective, too. I seen him snooping round old Buzby's desk. I only wish I wasn't dependin' on the old feller's good opinion to keep me solid with Sandman, I could tell a thing or two, but there ain't no use. The old man thinks the sun rises and sets in Buzby's ear."

"What could you tell?" I asked.

"Oh, no matter."

"Have another drink?"

"Well, I don't mind," he said, and after that I treated to cigars and made myself as pleasant as possible, bound to work it out of him before I got through.

And I succeeded. We were seated at a table talking confidentially in a little while, and I was flattering myself on my shrewdness in drawing young Spencer out.

It happened that he had seen in old Buzby's desk a false key to the outer door of the freight room, which was supposed to be entirely in charge of the freight superintendent.

"I tell you what it is, fellers," he added, "if we could only manage to get that key and slip in there some night, I have a key what would open his desk, and I'm sure we'd find something among his papers to prove that he's the one who is prigging money from the safe."

I jumped at the idea.

"Get me the key for an hour," I said, "and I'll have another made."

"Great scheme!" cried Jim Gleason. "If you do that we may catch him in the very act. Look here, Hen, I may as well tell you a secret. Mr. Kean is a detective. He's put in the office to watch us."

"Shut up with your nonsense!" I cried. "I only want to help you fellows—that's all."

"Don't deny it," persisted Gleason.

"I might have guessed as much," said Spencer. "I never seen a sharper fellow than you are, Sam Kean. Don't you fret. I'll snake the key out of old Buzby's desk while he's at lunch to-morrow. We'll have him where the wool is short and don't you forget it. It'll serve him just right too, for all his impudence to me."

"How much has he taken altogether?" I asked.

"Why he reports that $500 is missing so far," was Spencer's reply, "but as he's doing the stealing himself, how is one going to tell?"

After that I did not attempt to deny to these two that I was in the office as a spy.

They got the key and I had the duplicate made.

Thursday night was set for the execution of our little plan, for the reason that Spencer pretended to have been told by the old bookkeeper that he was going out of town that night.

"I'll bet you what you like it's only a dodge," he said. "That's the night he intends to make his next haul."

I was in high feather. I had no orders to go to the office and report to you so I didn't go.

"Wait till I surprise Mr. Brady by dragging Buzby to the New Church street station," I said to myself, for we three had agreed to do that very thing, provided we caught him in the store.

When the store closed that evening I slipped down-stairs to try my key in the lock of the freight-room door.

All hands had gone, or at least I supposed they had, so I was awfully startled at having a slim young fellow with black hair and determined-looking face suddenly pop up from behind some cases and ask me what the mischief I was doing there.

Really I forget what excuse I made, but I know I lit out as soon as I could, and made the best of my way up-stairs.

When I met Gleason and Spencer at a certain beer saloon in Greenwich street at eleven o'clock that night I told them about it, and could see that they looked worried.

"That's the new hand, Jack Rody," said Jim.

"I hope he ain't one of Buzby's pals," added Hen, "but I wouldn't be one mite surprised if he was."

Now I thought this was nonsense, and I said so. We got to talking about other things, and there the matter dropped.

"Time's up, boys," said Jim at last, just as the clock struck twelve. "We'd better slip round there now. There's just one thing that worries me though."

"What's that?" asked Hen.

"Suppose the cop catches us trying to enter the store."

"Well," replied Gleason. "Sam can fix that. He's got his shield I suppose."

"I've got no shield," I answered, this disagreeable possibility occurring to me for the first time.

But I was a good deal worried. I felt that it would be simply sickening to be arrested for burglary and have to send for you to get me out.

No such trouble occurred, however.

We watched our chance and slipped in through the back door of the Eagle Line office without the slightest difficulty.

It was not until we got the door shut and locked that I began to wonder what we were going to do for a light.

"Oh, I looked out for that," whispered Jim. "I've got a dark lantern."

He pulled it out, lit it and flashed it round him. There was no sign of Jack Rody, though I must confess I half expected to see him spring up from behind the cases again.

"Old Buz ain't here, that's one thing sure," whispered Gleason, when we got up-stairs into the office.

"We'll lay for him an hour or so, anyhow," replied Spencer.

"Mebbe he's been here already," suggested Jim.

"Suppose we open the safe and see if he's taken anything?" said Spencer, after a moment.

Now I give you my word, Mr. Brady, that this was the first I began to suspect there was anything wrong.

"Open the safe!" I exclaimed. "How are you fellows going to open the safe? What do you mean?"

"We mean this," hissed Jim, turning suddenly upon me, "we are tired of playing a dangerous game for small stakes. There's a thousand dollars in that safe to-night and we intend to have it, and leave you here to be pulled in as the thief."

I was thunderstruck. I saw it all.

"You've been playing me for a sucker," I blurted out. "I'll show you——"

"No you won't!" breathed Spencer, drawing a revolver and thrusting it in my face. "We have been playing you for just what you are. You pretend to be a detective! Bah! you're nothing but a little squirt, anyhow. We'll fix you. Here, Jim, give him his drink."

I fought like a tiger, never heeding the revolver, for I was sure they wouldn't shoot. Still I did not dare to make any outcry, for that would be sure to bring matters to a crisis.

It was all over in a minute. They had me down, and, while Gleason held me, Spencer got a rope out of his desk and tied me. Then Jim forced my mouth open, while his companion poured a lot of whisky down my throat, almost strangling me. I seemed to be entirely powerless to help myself.

Then I yelled like a good fellow.

All it amounted to was to cause them to jam a handkerchief in my mouth.

Never before nor since have I been a prey to such terrible feelings as I endured while I lay there and watched those two scoundrels open that safe.

Spencer was the one who had the key—a ridiculous old thing made up of a number of steel prongs which fitted in a slot.

I thought then and I still think that it served Sandman just right to be robbed, for trusting his money in such an old-fashioned affair.

Well, they opened it and they took the money from the cash-drawer, shaking the bills in my face in triumph.

"They'll find you here in the morning," sneered Gleason. "Mebbe they'll believe your story, and mebbe they won't. Anyhow your goose on the detective force is cooked. Next time you try to pump a fellow, go at it in the right way."

Of course I could say nothing—only stare helplessly.

I heard them laugh, I saw them move toward the basement door.

Then all of a sudden I saw the door fly open, and a determined voice shouted:

"Drop that money, gents, and the shooter along with it, or I'll drop you!"

It was Jack Rody, the new freight clerk.

His face was pale, but determined, as he stood there covering those two rascals with a cocked revolver in each hand, and to my further surprise I saw that his hair was not black now, but red.

Then I knew him.

It was David Doyle, the young fellow I had met in your office the day I first called.

Did we capture them?

Well, we just did.

Rather, I should say, Dave Doyle did it.

He made them release me, and then we took them to the station together, and next day Jim Gleason confessed that he and Spencer had done all the stealing.

You remember the end of it. They turned out to be a couple of worthless fellows and went up to the Elmira Reformatory in the end.

You were not very hard on me for the ridiculous way in which I had managed the affair—not half as hard as you might have been.

That's the story of my first case, Mr. Brady, and it taught me a lesson which I never forgot. Yours truly,

Sam Kean.

Note.—I may as well add that I knew all about that midnight business from the first.

No sooner had Sam Kean told me of the conversation he had had with Jim Gleason than I suspected the fellow, and put an experienced man to watch him nights.

I soon found that he and Spencer were inseparable companions; that they were drunkards and gamblers, and capable of committing any crime.

Kean had made a blunder very common with beginners in the detective business. He had not properly weighed the evidence, and had become a cat's-paw of the real criminal through allowing himself to be flattered.

I didn't blame him a bit.

When I first began to go about as a detective, I fell into a similar trap several times.

I was so sure Gleason and Spencer were doing the stealing, that I would have arrested them on suspicion and forced a confession out of them, had it not been that I wanted Sam Kean to understand just how foolish he had really been.

Well, he found out—don't make any mistake about that. A more thoroughly taken down individual you never saw.

After that he was willing enough to receive all the instructions I had a mind to give him.

You see I got Doyle into the freight-room at the end of the week, just as I told him I would, but Dave's appearance was altered by a black wig, and Sam never guessed who it was. Besides that I was in the cellar and came to the rescue at the proper moment.

It was Dave and I who took those two young scoundrels around to the New Church street station, or rather I did the most of it, for Dave had all he could do to take care of Sam.

Do you notice that my account of the end of the affair differs slightly from his? You will observe that he don't mention me at all?

Well, no wonder. The poor fellow was so drunk that he did not know which end he was standing on that night.

He says they forced liquor down his throat after he was bound. I know this to be true, for Dave saw them doing it through the key-hole; but I'm afraid Sam had taken several drinks before, or the stuff would not have had the effect upon him that it did.

Now this brings me to another and most important point—one that a young man in starting upon the career of a detective has got to pay more attention to than anything else.

As a detective you will often be thrown into positions where you have got to drink.

Now a drinking detective is but a poor worthless creature, as a rule. Then what are you going to do?

Here, again, no rule can be laid down. You must be guided by your constitution, by your conscience, by circumstances.

If you allow liquor to get control of you be very sure you will not be able to control your man. To think this is to make a great mistake.

Great criminals are seldom drunkards. If they lead you to drink, it is only that they may get the best of you in some way or other.

Still, to refuse absolutely, would be to excite suspicion, which leaves you between two fires, as it were.

I can only warn you—I cannot dictate.

The best way is to plead that liquor never agrees with you—too much never agrees with any one—and stick to temperance drinks.

If you feel that you must drink, make your drinks as small as possible and as few.

Some detectives have a knack of slyly turning their glass into the cuspidore or on the floor; others make it a rule to call for gin and then fill another glass with an equal amount of water; both the gin and the water being white they drink the latter and pretend to taste the gin.

These tricks may work satisfactorily if your man is under the influence himself, but if he is sober you are pretty sure to get caught at it and have your plans spoiled.

Whisky may have helped some detectives to make captures, and procure information which could never have been obtained without its aid; but on the other hand it has ruined thousands of young men who have set out to follow our business, and sent them to a drunkard's grave.

CHAPTER II
CAUGHT BY A HAT

Very often a little thing will furnish a clew and bring the criminal into the hands of the law, where all the shrewdness and vigilance in the world proves at fault.

The older I grow, the more firmly I believe that circumstances have a great deal to do with the success of some detectives. You may call it Providence, luck or whatever name you like.

You may lay out your plans in the most careful manner, but you seldom follow them as you originally propose.

Indeed, a detective who cannot break one of his rules and change his mind to suit the occasion, can never hope to be a success.

Little things, sudden ideas which seize hold of your mind, often lead you to results which the best formed plans could never do. Such has ever been my experience, and such also is the experience of my old pupil, Dave Doyle, who began to study under me at about the same time as Sam Kean.

Dave was a smart fellow, and a born detective, although a young man of no education at all, and for this reason unfitted for certain kinds of detective work.

Let me introduce one case in particular where Dave succeeded by following a sudden idea which seized hold of me. Later on Dave began to get ideas of his own.

I will let him tell the story himself.

Dave Doyle's First Case

When Mr. Philander Camm defaulted and ran away with $100,000 of the funds of the Bakers' Bank there was the biggest kind of a row.

A big reward was offered to any detective who would get him, and there seemed to be a chance that some one might earn it, for it was believed that the thief hadn't left New York.

I had just gone to work for Old King Brady then, and when I read the account in the papers I says to myself:

"I wish I could scoop in that reward."

I went up to the office that morning and spoke to Mr. Brady about it.

"Well," he says, "and if you did get him the reward wouldn't be yours by rights, but mine. Ain't you working for me?"

Now I hadn't looked at the thing that way, but I saw right off he was right.

"I'd like to get it for you then," I says.

"That's another part of speech," says he, "and maybe you can. I ain't got time to work up the case myself. Go ahead and see what you can do. If anything comes out of it I won't be mean."

"Do you mean it?" says I.

"Of course I do," says he. "You've got to take up a big case some time, and this will be a good one to begin with. You'll have every detective of any account against you, though. There ain't one chance in forty that you'll succeed."

Wasn't that encouraging?

But Old King Brady always did put things straight and call a spade a spade.

"What shall I do?" I asked him.

"Don't ask me," he says. "Make up some plan for yourself."

"I s'pose he'll try and get away by some of the railroads?" I says. "I might go and watch for him at the depot."

"Can you watch all the depots at once, Doyle?" he says, laughing. "Then there's the steamboats, too, and you know he might take a notion to walk."

I saw at once that he was right; then I asked him again what he'd do if he was in my place, and owned right up that I had no ideas.

He thought a few minutes, and then he said:

"Where does this man Camm live?"

"Don't know," I says. "The paper says he is a bachelor, and used to live in Forty-sixth street, but he gave up his room three weeks ago."

"Where did he come from?"

"Paper says he was born in Middlebury, Vermont," I says.

Then he went and got a geography and looked on the map.

"If he came from Middlebury he knows all about Canada," he says, "and he'll be sure to steer north if he hasn't gone already. If I was you I'd go up to the Grand Central Depot, and ask the man who sells the sleeping car berths if any one of his description has engaged a berth for to-night or last night. It's most likely he's gone."

"But he was seen at one o'clock this morning in the Fifth Avenue Hotel," I says.

"How do you know?" he says. "Because the papers say so? That's no proof. Just like as not that was all a put up job. Go up to the depot first of all, Doyle, and tell the fellow in the office I sent you. He knows me."

Well, I went.

I had a good description of the defaulter from the papers, but bless you! I didn't need it.

The fellow in the sleeping-car office was fly and right up to business. He knew all about it before I got there, but the worst of it was he'd told what he knew to two other fellows before he told me.

"That man engaged lower 10 for to-night," he says, "in the Montreal express. You won't be able to do nothing about it though. There's two ahead of you watching already. They think his taking the berth is only a blind, and that he'll go up on one of the day trains."

I was that disappointed that I could have cried when I left the office, for there stood Ed Duffy and old man Pease a-laughing at me. You see I'd been introduced to both of them by Mr. Brady, and they knew just who I was.

"Say, young feller," says Duffy, "you just go back and tell Old King Brady that he'd better come himself instead of sending a kid like you. 'Twon't make no difference, though. The fellow will be here in half an hour. He's going to take the ten o'clock train."

Wasn't I mad?

You'd just better believe I was.

When I went back to Mr. Brady, though, he only laughed at me.

"What do you 'spose them fellows do for a living?" he says. "They are up to their business as well as you or me."

"I 'spose I may as well give it up," I says.

"Not at all," says he. "Wouldn't do nothing of the sort. I don't believe they're going to get him just because they happen to be laying for him, and if you do you're a fool."

"Why, don't you think he's off for Montreal?" I says.

"Yes," says he, "of course, but not that way. The taking of that berth in his own name is a dead give away. He'll never go over the Central road."

"What way, then?" I says.

"How do I know?" says he, "but I've got an idea."

I asked him what it was, and he told me to go down to the bank and try and find out where Mr. Camm had been living for the last few weeks.

"But I can't find out that," I says. "Others have tried it and failed. How can I hope to succeed?"

"Never you mind, Dave, you go," he says. "Something tells me you will succeed."

So I went.

I had a note from Mr. Brady to the bank president, and he treated me civil enough.

"I don't know where he lived, and no one else don't neither," he says. "He's kept himself in hiding for more'n three weeks."

"Ain't there anything here what belongs to him?" I asked, for you see I'd been figuring it all out on the way down to the bank and it come to me somehow that this was what I wanted to say.

"Why there's lots of things," says the president. "There's his old coat and two or three old hats, and an umbrella and a couple of pair of old shoes, but what does that amount to?"

"Let me see 'em?" says I.

He showed me a clothes closet where the things were along with a lot of other rubbish. I couldn't make nothing out of them, although I examined everything carefully till I come to one hat—a plug—which looked to me to be new.

Now you may laugh just as much as you please, but I knowed right away as soon as I took the hat into my hands that I'd found what I was looking for.

"This is a new one," I says to the president, who stood right behind me.

"Maybe. I don't know nothing at all about it," he says.

"But it is," says I. "It ain't never been worn at all. Did it come to the bank from the maker, or did he bring it?"

"You'll have to ask Camm; I'll never tell you," he says.

Well, now I'd just like to have had the chance to ask Camm, you bet.

But there wasn't any show then, so I asked the man whose name was in the hat. It was Silverstein in the Bowery, a little dried-up Jew.

Now I expected nothing but to get fired out as soon as ever I went into the store, so I just tried a little dodge.

I went in with a rush.

"Say!" I says. "Mr. Brady wants to know who you sold this hat to?"

Silverstein looked as though he'd like to eat me. They say he sells policy slips as well as hats, and I reckoned on that to make him afraid.

"What Brady?" he says.

"Old King Brady, the detective," says I.

"Mein freund, how I can be ogspeged to know efery hat vat I sells. Who I sells him to—huh?"

"Mr. Brady don't want to know who you sell all your hats to," I say, "he only wants to know who you sold this one to."

Silverstein took the hat and examined it closely.

"Vell, I tells you," he said, slowly. "I understand vat Mr. Brady vants. Dis hat I sells to an old gustomer vat's named Camm."

"Yes, yes. But where did you deliver it; or did he take it with him when he bought it?"

"I send him," says Silverstein. It was like pulling teeth to get a word out of him, but I saw that sooner or later he meant to tell.

"Where did you send the hat?"

"To Brooklyn."

"Whereabouts in Brooklyn?"

He looked in his order book and told me it was a certain number on Rockaway avenue, which, by the way, was in that part of Brooklyn then known as East New York.

At that time it was all lots out there, with only a few straggling houses and plenty of geese, goats and pigs. It's a little better now, but as it was then I wouldn't have lived there if they'd given me a house rent free.

I went out to East New York late that afternoon, for I wanted to talk to Old King Brady first off, and I had to wait for him to come in.

"You're on the right track," he said. "Go, and good luck go with you. Do you think you can arrest him if you happen to get the chance?"

"Well, now, there'll be a rough fight if he gets away from me," I says.

"Go on," he says, "and don't let me see you again till you have something to report."

Now that kind of worried me, for I didn't feel at all sure that I was going to find my man just because I'd got the number of the house where he sent the hat.

On the way out to East New York I got to thinking suppose I was the defaulter what would I do?

Would I come back to the city and run the risk of being taken if I was hiding out there in the lots?

"Not much!" I says to myself. "I'd just keep right on by the Long Island railroad, get to Greenport and cross over to New London, where I could take the train on the Northern railroad straight to Montreal."

Why, it was a splendid chance. The more I thought about it the more I seemed to see how splendid it was.

"He's done it! I'll just bet a dollar he's done it!" I thought. "The taking of that berth on the Central was a blind just as Old King Brady said. He's gone already, I make no doubt."

However, I kept right on.

You never seen such forlorn houses as these were in all your born days.

There was a whole row of them, many as a dozen altogether. The windows were all broke and the doors bursted in, and in one or two places the folks in the neighborhood had carried away a whole lot of the weather-boards to burn.

There was only two houses in the whole row what had folks living into them, and one of them was the very number I wanted.

I tell you I was all in a shake when I knocked on the door—there wasn't no bell.

When the woman came to the door I had my little story all ready.

"Here's Mr. Camm's hat, mum," I says, "I came over from Mr. Silverstein's in the Bowery. There's a dollar to pay."

"No, there ain't!" she blurted right out mad like, then she switched up all of a sudden and looked scared like.

"I don't know what yer talkin' about," she says. "There ain't nobody of that name here. You must have got the wrong house."

I was half way through the door, and tried to get the whole way in, but she sorter got in front of me and worked me out into the airy.

"You needn't try to crowd in here," she says. "Get off with your lies and your hat."

"Say, you don't expect me to lug that hat-box all the way back to the Bowery," I says. "Mr. Silverstein has sent hats to this house before, and I guess you can't fool me if you try."

But I want you to understand that she would slam the door in my face, and she did.

Just as I was backing out of the yard I heard a slight rattle of the blinds at one of the upper windows.

I looked up and caught a glimpse of a man's face looking at me through the slats.

"Say, is this your hat, mister?" I hollered.

The face disappeared.

"By thunder, I've a good mind to chuck the thing in the lot sooner than lug it all the way back to New York," I hollered again, loud enough for any one to hear.

Then I walked off like I was mad.

"That's him!" I thought to myself. "That's Camm."

Now, how did I know?

Couldn't tell you if I was to try, but I did know. I never had no more doubt about Camm being in that house from that minute than I have that I'm Dave Doyle.

And I was right.

Wait till you hear what I did, and you'll see.

I did chuck away the hat-box—I had no further use for it. I threw it in a lot, and went over to the Howard House, where the train on the Long Island Railroad used to start from and stop in them days, and looked at a time-table. Right away I seen that there was a train for Greenport at half past eight. It was then pretty near six o'clock.

Back I goes and lays around the lots a-watching.

Part of the time I was up at the end of the row, hiding in one of the unoccupied houses. Part of the time I kept between them and the Howard House, for I felt dead sure my man would come out sooner or later.

At quarter to eight I was round in front, hiding behind a tree and watching the front door, when all at once it came flashing over me, "What's to hinder him from going out the back way and cutting across lots?"

I run up the street to the end of the row, where I could get a view of the lots in the rear.

Sure enough!

There was a man all muffled up to the eyes in a big ulster coat, traveling across lots toward the Howard House, carrying a black leather grip sack in his hand.

Was it Mr. Camm?

It might have been him, or, for that matter, anybody else. How did I even know he came out of that house at all?

I cut after him, not running, of course, but walking fast enough to gain on him some.

This I could see was making him nervous, and he began to walk all the faster. I took it for a good sign that it was really Camm.

"If he buys a ticket for Greenport, I'll grab him," says I to myself.

I took a good look at him, wondering how much fight there was into him. He wasn't a very big feller, and I was considered a perfect terror down in the fourth ward, so I wasn't afraid.

"I'm good for two like him," thinks I, and I pinned my shield on inside my coat, so as to show if a crowd tried to hustle me. But, gracious! you never know how things is going to come out.

We'd got pretty well over to the Howard House by this time, and right ahead, between him and the station, was a lot of empty freight-cars standing.

He struck around the cars on one side and me on the other. When I got onto the platform there wasn't nothing of him to be seen.

Thunderation, wasn't I mad!

"He's given me the slip," I thought. "He's tumbled to my little racket," and I ran around on the other side of the cars, thinking he must have dodged back.

But he wasn't there. I couldn't see nothing of him no where. I bet you I was just about the sickest fellow in East New York then.

Had he slipped into one of the freight cars?

I thought so, and I was just going to look when all of a sudden the train came thundering in.

It was a sort of a switch train. It ran down from Jamaica and then went right back again, passengers changing cars at Jamaica for the regular trains on the Long Island road.

Now I hardly knew what to do.

The conductor was yelling all aboard, and there wasn't a minute to lose.

The train, as it stood, was right close alongside these empty freight cars, and it would have been an easy matter for a man to step from one to the other.

"That's what he means to do," thinks I, and I jumped into the forward car, which was nearest to where I stood, and began to hurry through the train.

He wasn't in that car, nor in the next.

Just as I crossed the platform to the car the train started, and I began to think he'd given me the slip altogether, for he wasn't in the last car either, as far as I could see.

I ran through the car as fast as I could with my mind made up to jump off the platform. When I got to the rear door and was just about to open it, I suddenly saw my man jump from one of the empty freight cars as we passed and land on the platform right before my eyes.

You oughter see me open that door!

I was out on the platform in a second. He gave one look at me and seemed to know just what I wanted, too, for he out with a gun and rammed it right in my face.

"Blast you! I'll never be taken alive!" he hissed.

But I gave the shooter one clip and sent it flying off the train.

"Help! Murder!" he yelled as we went sweeping past the platform of the Howard House.

I grabbed him by the throat and had him down in a minute. Two men jumped into the car and grabbed me.

"He's a thief! He's trying to rob me!" he hollered.

"I'm a detective—he's a defaulter! Help me, gents!" I said, as cool as I could.

Well, we got him—that's all there is to it.

More than that we got the boodle—a hundred thousand clear. It was all in the bag.

They stopped the train and we took him off. One of the fellers what had jumped on was a policeman, and he helped me take him to the East New York station. We found a ticket for Greenport on him and a time-table of the Northern New London Railroad. I never had the least doubt but what he'd a-got through safe to Montreal if it hadn't been for Mr. Brady sending me out to East New York that night.

As for the reward, Old King Brady scooped it in, and a big laugh we had on Detective Duffy and the old man Pease, who hung around the Grand Central till midnight watching for their man who never came.

"But it was only guess work after all," says Old King Brady, when he gave me a big lump of money out of the reward a couple of weeks later on.

Very true.

It was all guess work.

But there's something funny about Old King Brady and his guesses.

Somehow or other he manages to guess right nine times out of ten.

Note.—Now this case is only a sample of a good many.

I don't know why I got the impression that Mr. Camm would try to reach Montreal by the Long Island road, but I had it as well as Dave Doyle. I don't know why I get half my impressions, but I always follow them, and they don't often lead me astray.

One thing in particular is very strongly illustrated by this case which a young detective should always remember, and it is something which the majority of our oldest hands are pretty apt to forget.

Don't trust to appearances. They are pretty sure to lead you astray.

Put yourself in the place of the criminal. Try and fancy how you would act if you were placed in his position, and be guided in what you do thereby.

Now here is a rule and it is a good one—yet it is not always safe to follow it.

There is another thing to be considered—the intelligence of the criminal.

Mr. Camm was an intelligent man—emphatically so.

Was it to be supposed that an intelligent man making off with a hundred thousand dollars would openly engage a berth in a sleeping car in his own name?

Decidedly not. It was a blind on the face of it. If I had been in his place I would never for an instant have expected any one to be deceived by so transparent an action, but I took another thing into consideration. Mr. Camm was not as well used to the methods of criminals as I was, therefore I did not blame him for thinking that he might deceive the detectives by his little game.

And was he so far out of the way either?

Evidently not, since he did fool Detective Duffy and my friend Mr. Pease completely, and this brings me to another point.

Some detectives can never see beyond the length of their noses. They seize upon the first clew offered and hold to it like grim death, never stopping to think that what they consider a clew may be only a bait.

Such men can never make their mark in this business, no matter how long they stick at it. They are constantly getting into hot water, and have only themselves to blame.

Now a word more about my young friend Doyle.

He is sharp, shrewd and persevering, but in spite of it he is only adapted to certain kinds of work, and can never hope to become a great success.

Why?

Simply because he is not possessed of all the qualifications I have laid down.

Dave lacks education. He has never in his life moved in good society. Often it becomes necessary for a detective to disguise himself as a high-toned gentleman and move in the best society of the land.

To send Dave Doyle on such a mission would be worse than nonsense. He would fail before he had the chance to begin.

Take a case where it is necessary to track a man through the slums and Dave hasn't his equal. Take a case of shadowing where untiring vigilance and bulldog pertinacity are the principal requirements, and he is there, too, but in disguises he's just nowhere. That freckled face and red hair of his is a dead give away—you understand what I mean.

To be a successful detective a man must be a thorough gentleman in every sense of the word.

A gentleman can adapt himself to the lowest as well as those who are higher in the social scale, but the case cannot be reversed.

There are many cases where even I would be useless.

Suppose, for instance, it were necessary to worm our way into the confidence of a young lady. What could an old man like me hope to accomplish in a case like that?

Nothing, of course.

It would be necessary to have an assistant, either a good-looking young man or a woman.

So you see no detective can cover the whole ground, and you must not only know how to choose your assistants, but how to use them to the best advantage.

That's where the all important qualification of good judgment and common sense comes in.

CHAPTER III
SHADOWING

The art of shadowing is perhaps one of the most difficult things a detective has to learn.

I mean, of course, difficult to become a good shadow — of the ordinary species, dogging the steps of the suspected criminal, giving themselves away at every possible opportunity, we have plenty and to spare.

It is not an easy matter to shadow some men unsuspected, and yet there are others whom one could follow half around the world and never a suspicion aroused.

Thus the ease or difficulty in the case of shadowing depends as much on the subject as upon the shadower; still a good shadower can accomplish wonders even with a difficult subject if he only gives his mind to his work.

The best shadows are men of common minds and insignificant appearance, who will pass readily without special notice in a crowd.

Men with strong minds and intense will power are apt, by the very intensity of their thought, to impress their subject with their presence, which he soon detects and the usefulness of the detective is gone.

Now for these very reasons I do not consider myself a good shadower, although long experience has enabled me to become quite expert at the business nevertheless.

I am too tall; my appearance is too marked.

I can, it is true, change my appearance by disguises, but I cannot add to or take from my stature, and my victim soon falls to wondering why so many tall men keep following him — from that moment my usefulness is gone.

I always choose medium sized men with light brown hair and mild blue eyes for shadows, when I can get them. A boy makes a splendid shadow. I have used them a great deal, and often very successfully. A woman if she is shrewd makes the very best of shadows for a man, but a very bad one for another woman.

My experience has shown me that most men seldom notice plain women in the street, although the contrary is generally believed to be the case.

Of course in all this I allude to city work. Out in the country it is altogether different. There the shadow must worm himself into the confidence of his subject and travel with him. He will surely lose him if he don't.

And this is often done, and most successfully.

I once sent a young man all over South America with a defaulting bank cashier. It was necessary to inveigle the fellow upon United States soil before he could be arrested.

To do this was difficult. My man first struck him in the city of Mexico and made his acquaintance at a hotel, taking pains to get an introduction to him which put him on a proper footing at the start.

For over a year he stuck to him and they grew to be like brothers.

They visited Brazil, Chili, Buenos Ayres and Peru; eating together, sleeping together, and all that sort of thing.

Long before the year was over the defaulter confessed the whole story to my man. He had taken $100,000 and had it all with him in gold and bills of exchange except what had been spent in his wanderings.

One day while at Callao, Peru, my man induced him to visit an American man-of-war then lying in the harbor.

This was the opportunity for which he had been so long seeking, and he immediately revealed himself and placed the defaulter under arrest, for to all intents and purposes they were then on American soil.

"My God! Jim, you can't mean it!" the poor wretch exclaimed. "And I loved you so!"

Then he covered his face with his hands and cried like a child.

He brought him back on the man-of-war and the bank recovered $60,000 by the operation; the balance had been used up for expenses, and went to pay me the cost of the detective's trip, which I personally advanced.

Now this was a shrewd piece of work. I admired my man for it from a business standpoint, but from a moral one I despised him.

I never could have done what he did in the world. It ain't my nature. It needs a consummate hypocrite to successfully play such a role as that.

But such men are necessary to the detective force, and we must have them. I suppose all my readers are aware that we make use of thieves, gamblers and other hard characters very often to assist us in our work.

We have got to do this. We could not get along at all if we didn't. Yet we never trust them one inch further than our interests are concerned; if we did we should get fooled every time.

So you see there are shadows and shadows, and the only rule I can lay down is the rule of common sense.

In shadowing use your judgment. Employ such means as circumstances seem to demand. Disguises will help you—are often entirely necessary, but it don't do to put too much dependence on them. Common sense, quickness of thought, and a glib tongue will do more for the shadow than the best disguise ever made.

I remember a very clever piece of double shadowing accomplished shortly after Sam Kean began to study with me.

As I sent him west soon after it occurred it became necessary for him to write out a deposition of the case to be used by the district attorney in preparing the trial of this criminal. I happened to come across a copy of that document in my desk the other day, and may as well incorporate it here. I will call it

The Story of the Jewel Thief

On a certain afternoon in February, I was sitting in Mr. Brady's private office, waiting to receive instructions, when the boy brought in two cards. They bore the names of Mr. Marcus Welton and Mr. J. Denby Opdyke.

"Two high-toned ducks." I immediately thought.

"Skip into that closet, Kean," old King Brady whispered to me. "I want you to have a good look at these fellows, and listen to what they say. You know where the peep-hole is, or you ought to, for I showed you the other day."

I knew, and in a moment I had my eye glued against it.

I was not mistaken in my estimate of the visitors. They were a couple of dudes of the most pronounced sort.

Welton was short and sallow, with big bulging eyes, a drawling voice. He looked what he was—a society fool.

His companion, however, was quite different. He was a tall, handsome fellow, with brown hair, shrewd gray eyes, and a determined mouth; yet there was something about his face which repelled me at once.

Both men were dressed in the most pronounced fashion of the day, and bore every evidence of possessing abundant means.

"Aw, Mr. Bwady, you got my note left here yestawday, I dessay," drawled Welton.

"I did, sir," replied the detective in his usual quick way. "Be seated, please."

They accepted the invitation and Welton continued:

"What I want to see you about is a private mattaw. For some time past there have been wobbowies of jewelry in some of our best society. These wobbowies always take place on the occasion of parties or balls."

"Yes, sir," said Old King Brady as he paused.

"We want you to catch the thief," said Mr. Welton. "My—aw—mother has been wobbed of a lot of diamonds. They were taken when she gave her ball a week ago. I want them—aw—wecovered. My fwiend, Mr. Opdyke, has a fwiend who has been wobbed. Mrs. Porthouse, widow of Admirwal Porthouse of the Navy. No doubt you knew the admiral. She has lost diamonds too—she wants them wecovered."

"And very valuable ones they were, I assure you, sir," put in Mr. Opdyke, who did not lisp.

"But have you no clew to the thief, gentlemen? Nothing to go by?" asked the detective.

No, they had absolutely nothing to offer. They wanted the thief caught and the diamonds recovered—they had no ideas beyond that.

Old King Brady thought a moment.

"When does society give its next ball, gentlemen?" he asked.

"To-night at Mrs. Lispenard's," answered Mr. Welton, promptly.

"Very good. To-night I will have a detective at Mrs. Lispenard's, and we will see what can be done."

"Give him a letter to me and I'll post him," said Mr. Opdyke. "My office is at No. — Wall street. Let him come before three."

"Very good," replied Old King Brady, and they left.

Now I fully expected that I was going to be sent out on that case, but I wasn't.

When I came out of the closet Old King Brady had nothing to say about it, and didn't allude to the matter for nearly five weeks—in fact till after Lent.

One day he called me aside and said, "You remember those two dudes who called on me that day you hid in the closet?"

"Yes," said I.

"I sent a man to Opdyke," he said, "and just as I supposed there was nothing taken that night."

"Surely you don't suspect Mr. Opdyke gave you away?" I exclaimed.

"I do. He may not have done it intentionally, but I'm certain he did it. I also have other suspicions. I've been quietly looking into this case."

"And your suspicions are?"

"No matter. I want you to take a hand in it, Kean."

"All right, sir," I said, willing enough.

"To-night Mrs. Welton, the mother of that young squirt, gives a ball. You are to be present. You will be admitted without question, for the servant who tends the door will be one of my men."

"And then, sir?"

"And then you'll catch the jewel thief if you can," he replied, somewhat testily.

"But have you no instructions?" I asked.

"No, sir. How can I have instructions when I don't know anything about the matter? Do the best you can. I select you because you are a gentleman and have moved in good society. I expect you to catch that jewel thief to-night Mr. Kean."

"But," I protested, "ain't you expecting too much?"

"That remains to be seen, sir."

"I thought Mrs. Welton's diamonds were stolen?"

"Bless my soul, sir!" he exclaimed, "the woman is worth four or five millions—don't you suppose she's bought new ones? Go, now, and do your very best."

I left the office feeling that I had shouldered a big responsibility.

Hurrying home I dressed in my swallow tail and took a cab to Mrs. Welton's. I had cards with all sorts of names engraved on them then. I remember the one I handed to the butler bore the name of Mr. Winfield Went. I eyed the man and saw at a glance that he was disguised. I thought I recognized him, but more on that matter later on.

Once by the door, of course I passed into the parlors unchallenged, my assumed name was announced, and Mrs. Welton greeted me most effusively. Whether she knew me or not for what I really was I cannot say.

Mr. Opdyke was there, and so was Marcus Welton, but I am sure neither of these gentlemen had the faintest suspicion that I was not straight.

The parlors were a perfect blaze of light; beautiful women and correctly attired men were moving in every direction; hidden behind a bank of flowers a noted orchestra discussed Lanner, Strauss, Offenbach, and other noted composers of that day.

Did I join in and dance?

Well, now, you may be very sure I did.

Fortunately there was no one present whom I knew, for Mrs. Welton's was several pegs higher than any house I had ever visited before.

"What in the world am I to do?" I kept thinking. "Where am I to begin?" It was a puzzler, but I hadn't learned the secret of patient waiting then.

After supper I strolled into the smoking-room.

There were a lot of gentlemen there, Mr. Opdyke among the rest.

I had no more than crossed the threshold than I perceived that they were talking about the jewel thief.

"He's given you one call, hasn't he, Welton?" asked a Mr. Dalledouze.

"Yaas," drawled Welton. "He got away with a lot, too. But my mother has weplaced them. She don't wear diamonds to-night, because she's afraid to show them, but there's ten thousand dollars' worth in her dressing-case up-stairs, all the same."

"Gad! I wouldn't blow about it if I was you then," spoke up a Mr. Partello. "Whoever the jewel thief is, be very sure he passes for a gentleman. He may be right among us now for all we know."

Then everybody looked at me because I was a stranger, and I haven't the least doubt that some of them put me down for the thief.

"He's bound to be caught sooner or later, though!" said Mr. Opdyke.

"Sure," replied Partello. "No balls given without detectives now, gentlemen."

"I'm surprised," I put in, "not to see one here to-night."

"How do you know there ain't one?" demanded Opdyke, putting his single glass into his eye, and staring at me.

"Is there one?" I asked, as innocent as you please.

"I know nothing about it," he said, shortly. I turned away, and began talking to a gentleman who stood near me. But I kept my eye upon everybody in the room.

"If the thief is here, he heard Welton's foolish boast about the diamonds," I reflected. "If he heard that he will try to get them, and there's no better chance than now, while the gentlemen are busy with their cigars."

I watched curiously to see who would be the first to leave the room, and made up my mind that I had got to do a little shadowing. I was right.

"Welton!" exclaimed Mr. Opdyke suddenly. "I don't want to hurt your feelings, old fellow, but these cigars of yours are not worth a continental."

"Bought 'em at Lark and Gilford's anyhow!" retorted Welton. "They cawst twenty dollars a hundred, by Jove, so they ought to be good."

"Pshaw! Price has got nothing to do with it," cried Opdyke. "Let me give you a cigar that I've struck. It's in my overcoat pocket. I'll fetch it in just one minute. You wait."

Now I had made up my mind to follow the first man who left the room, and consequently I started to follow Mr. Opdyke.

Of course I had to wait a moment for decency's sake, then I hurried out to the coat-room. I went straight, too.

Mr. Opdyke was not there.

"Where's that gentleman who was here a second ago, Sam?" I asked of the darky who had charge of the coats.

"Warn't no gemplum here, sah!" replied the fellow grinning, for I had tipped him a dollar.

"Sure?"

"Suah as death, sah."

I retreated. But I had not gone two steps before I met Mr. Opdyke coming along the hall.

"Got through smoking?" he asked, nodding pleasantly.

"Yes," I replied. "You were right about those cigars."

"Of course I was."

"Did you get those of yours?"

"Oh, yes. Just got them from my top coat. Have one?"

"Thank you."

I accepted the weed, but I knew that it didn't come from his coat.

"Madame," said I to Mrs. Welton, drawing her aside a few moments later. "I have a confession to make!"

"What is it, Mr. Went?" She was all smiles as she put the question, and when I informed her that I was a detective she didn't look a bit disturbed.

"Well, sir, what is it?" she asked. "I knew a detective was in the house, but I confess I did not suspect you."

"I want you to go immediately and look at your jewel case," I whispered.

She turned pale, and yet she ought to have expected it.

"You don't mean——" she began.

"But I do, though. Which is your room, madam?"

She told me.

It was close to the door of that room that I met Mr. Opdyke with his cigars.

Mrs. Welton took my advice.

"I'll wait for you at the foot of the stairs," I whispered.

In a moment she came back, looking paler still.

"Every diamond has been taken," she whispered, excitedly, "and you know the thief?"

"Pardon me, madam; I only suspect."

"Who?"

"No matter."

"Not—not my son?"

"Thank God, no, Mrs. Welton."

She looked relieved.

"Don't you arrest him here!" she said, hurriedly. "I'd rather lose the diamonds twice over than to have it occur in my house. I'll reward Mr. Brady handsomely if the jewels are recovered, but it must be done somewhere else."

She left me, and I at once got my hat and coat and hurried to the street.

As I passed out I noticed that there was another doorkeeper now, but I thought nothing of it at the time.

Did I suspect Opdyke then?

I did, and with reason.

When I started to go back to the smoking room he was in the coat room getting ready to leave. I did not stop to speak or delay a moment, but just tipped the darky a wink, got my coat and slid out ahead.

"I'll shadow that man," I thought. "It won't do to arrest him and get left."

Candidly, I hardly cared to undertake the job, for he was a big, powerful fellow and had Mr. Dalledouze with him.

I slipped across the street, changing my opera hat for a slouch felt, and putting on a false mustache.

There I stood behind a tree peering out and watching the steps of the Welton mansion with eager eyes.

I was disappointed when I saw them come out together, but it couldn't be helped.

It was then just one o'clock.

They passed me and never suspected, still talking about the cigars.

Then I glided after them and saw them enter the Brunswick. They went into the bar-room and so did I, but I simply passed in one door and out the other. They were drinking at the bar; that was enough to tell me that they meant to come out soon.

Opdyke came out alone ten minutes later. Afterward I learned that his companion lived at the hotel.

He started down Fifth avenue. I moved along on the other side of the way.

Once he looked round, and I knew that he was looking at me.

Did he suspect?

Evidently, for he crossed right over and managed to get behind me. I grew nervous, but there was no safe way but to keep straight on.

How keenly I listened to the ring of his footsteps I'll never tell you. I still heard them; he was coming toward me — not going back.

"He don't suspect," I muttered. "Perhaps, after all, I'm wrong."

Soon he passed me, for I had slackened my pace. He never turned his eyes, though, but just walked straight across the square, passed the Fifth Avenue Hotel, and I saw him stop and speak to a hack driver on the Twenty-third street side.

Now, here is where what Old King Brady called my fine work came in.[1] I saw Mr. Opdyke enter that hack, and I saw the driver leap on the box and whip up his horses, but I did not make the mistake of thinking that my man was inside.

Why?

Positively I can't tell. I was too far away to see the dodge, but I felt sure that he had passed through the hack, paying the fellow to drive off as he did.

Therefore, instead of running after the hack down Twenty-third street, as a fool would have done, I shot over to lower Fifth avenue, and was just in time to spy my man walking on ahead at a rapid pace.

He had crossed the street while I was watching the hack.

Now I felt that I had no ordinary person to deal with. He knew me, and he knew that I knew him.

Twice he looked around, but I took care to remain as much as possible in the shadow of the buildings, so he did not see me. While I walked I changed my hat for another and put on English side whiskers—then I was a different man.

Where was he going?

I had not long to wait without knowing.

He hurried down Fifth avenue to Waverly Place—along Waverly Place to a certain side street, running up the stoop of the corner house. Before I could reach the spot he had passed inside.

Had I lost him?

At first I thought so, and was wondering what I ought to do when a policeman came along.

I showed him my shield and told him what I was after.

"What's going on in there?" I asked, pointing to the house.

"Sure that's Mike Reed's," said the officer. "You must be a new hand at the business if you don't know Big Mike."

Now I didn't know Big Mike, and I said so, whereupon I was informed that the big one ran a little game. How well the fellow knew!

"Is it a tough place?" I asked.

"So, so," replied the officer.

I was too proud to ask him to help me. I was resolved to capture that man myself and take him to the station—something I had never done as yet.

But I am willing to admit that I was all in a tremble when I pulled Mike Reed's bell.

There was no trouble in getting in.

One sharp look on the part of the darky door-tender, and I was admitted.

There were quite a few persons in the lower rooms, and among them Mr. Opdyke. He was standing over the *rouge-et-noir* table, and had already taken a hand in the game.

I walked boldly up to the table and joined in.

Opdyke looked up at me as I bought the chips, but his glance was only momentary. It was quite evident that he did not suspect.

We played out four rounds, and to my astonishment I won.

I could see that Opdyke was getting worked up, and I threw down the cards and walked away.

I was deeply perplexed.

How could I accomplish my purpose without raising a scene?

There was one way which had suggested itself to me at the outset, and for want of a better plan I resolved to try that.

Now before I entered Big Mike's at all, I had walked around on the side street and taken a careful survey of the ground.

There was a low brick wall dividing the yard from the street, and a back piazza behind the house.

If I could only get him out into the back yard and through the side gate I thought, I shall be all right.

I knew it was make or break with me. If he was an innocent man, my detective career was as good as closed, for Opdyke was a lawyer and a member of a good New York family. Nothing short of finding the jewels in his possession would fill the bill.

Then I resolved to try the power of dollars and my official shield.

"Sam," I said, button-holing the darky in the hall.

"Yes, sir."

"Do you want to make ten dollars?"

"Yes, sir, you bet, ef it won't cost me my job."

"Do you see that tall, black-haired man in there?"

"Yes, sir."

"Know him?"

"Yes, sir. He often come here."

"Is he liberal to you?"

"Never give me a cent, sir."

"Look here, I'll give you ten dollars now if you do just as I say. It shan't cost you your job and I'll give you ten more. Sam, I'm a detective. I want that man, and I won't get him out of here without a row—see!"

Sam's eyes rolled until only the whites could be seen. I had displayed my shield.

"What can I do, sir?" he asked, pocketing the bill.

"That back door," I whispered, "is it ever used?"

"Always, to go out of after midnight, sir."

"And the gate?"

"The gate opens on the inside, sir, wif a spring latch."

"Sam," I continued, "you open that gate, let me out the back way, and then call out that gentleman, and tell him quietly that some one is on the back stoop who wants to see him. If he comes out, you'll find a ten dollar bill on the stoop just as soon as we're gone. Be sure you lock the door after he passes through."

When I told Old King Brady about that scheme, he laughed, and said it was a crazy one, and might have got me into a heap of trouble.

Very good. I'm willing he should think so. It succeeded all the same.

Sam opened the gate, let me out on the stoop, and there I waited, ten dollar bill in hand.

It was only for a few moments I had to wait, but I just want you to understand that I got nervous. I was all in a shake when the door suddenly opened, and Mr. J. Dudley Opdyke, without a hat, stepped out.

"You!" he exclaimed. "What the devil do you want with me, sir, that you couldn't say inside?"

Bang went the door behind him, and the key was heard to turn in the lock.

I think he suspected the moment the door closed, but I didn't give him the chance to do anything—not even to say a word.

"I want you!" I hissed, covering him with my revolver, and clutching his arm with what Old King Brady calls my iron grip.

He never said a word, but just went for me.

In an instant my revolver was knocked out of my hand, and we, locked in each other's arms, went rolling down the stoop.

Then I thought he had me.

He was trying to get at his pistol—I had no other weapon than the one I had lost.

Everything seemed to depend then upon who happened to be the under dog.

Well, the under dog that time happened to be my humble self.

"I'll never be taken alive," he breathed, half rising and planting his knee on my breast.

I saw the glitter of his revolver. I saw him raise it—heard the cock click, when suddenly a firm voice now grown familiar to me spoke.

"Don't yer do it, boss. Drop that shooter or you're a dead duck. One—two——"

The revolver went ringing to the pavement, and through the gate a man came dashing with a cocked revolver in each hand. By that I would have known him if by nothing else.

It was Mrs. Welton's butler, but it was also Dave Doyle!

"Grab him!" he breathed.

I had already grabbed him.

"Snake him through the gate before the house gets onto us!" he added.

Well, in spite of the fight he showed we "snaked" him through the gate.

"What do you want?" Opdyke stammered, now completely cowed.

"These!" I exclaimed, pulling a jewel-case out of his inner pocket. "I haven't been shadowing you for nothing, my friend."

"Diamonds!" echoed Dave, holding him while I opened the case.

"I knowed we'd fetch him, Sam, soon as ever I seen you go out of the house and started on the shadow myself."

Well, we got him safely to the station-house, and then sent for Old King Brady.

After that I—but I think I've told my story about to the end, so I may just as well wind up right here.

Note:—Now, this is a case of double shadowing, and it illustrates also a great principle in detective science, (which is that when two men are earnestly working in a case, both determined to succeed) they will seemingly play into each other's hands.

I don't know how to explain it, but it's almost always so.

Dave Doyle told me next morning that he was just as certain that Sam Kean would try to get his man out by the back way as he ever was of anything.

How did he know it?

Now that is something I can't tell you—I can only say that the same thing has often happened to me.

You see I was inclined to suspect Opdyke, because I had taken the trouble to inquire into his habits, but I had no idea that Sam would get anything more than a clew that night.

Yet to make sure I had Doyle put on the door as butler, Mrs. Welton was perfectly informed of the whole plot.

As soon as Opdyke and his friend Dalledouze left the house, Dave, who had been alive to what was going on, followed them.

He shadowed Sam all the way to Big Mike's, and never gave himself away once.

How did he do it?

Why by keeping at a considerable distance and always in the shadow.

Of course one runs a risk of losing the game by doing this, but Dave took the chances and won.

If Sam's shadowing work was good, then Dave's was better, but if I had told either that the other one was working on the case I doubt if the result would have been so good.

You can't act out your true nature if you know some one is watching you all the time.

Sam had not the faintest idea that Dave Doyle was on the case until he sprang through Big Mike's back gate just in time to save his life, while Dave, who had been in the house all the afternoon, never knew that Sam was coming until he suddenly appeared at the door.

Before this Dave had selected Mr. Opdyke as the thief—I mean before the night of the party, because he had shadowed him to Big Mike's the day previous, and there saw him exhibit a set of diamond jewelry—pin, earrings, etc.—of great value, which Dave at once recognized as stolen goods.

That is why I hoped Sam would trap him, and that it would be valuable practice for him, I knew, so—but there I've said enough and need only add that after a long and weary trial Opdyke was convicted and sent to Sing Sing on a fifteen year sentence, which was all it amounted to, for he had powerful friends possessed of that mysterious influence "political pull."

Would you believe it? In less than six months I met Opdyke walking down Broadway with all the assurance you please.

"Hello!" I exclaimed, grabbing him by the arm unceremoniously, "how did you get out?"

"Go to thunder and find out!" he retorted, pulling away.

I wasn't to be put off that way, so I grabbed him again and let him understand that I meant business. I ran him around to headquarters in short order.

Well, what do you think it amounted to for me?

Confidentially, let me tell you, that it came pretty near depriving me of my own position on the police force.

Next day I met Mr. Opdyke sailing down Wall street.

I didn't arrest him that time. He is now a noted stock operator and is believed to be a millionaire, but I know him to be a rascal from the crown of his head to the soles of his feet.

That's the way the efforts of the detective are often brought to nought. It is an outrage and a shame that it should be so, but so it is.

"Didn't I send you to the island for six months last week?" asked my friend Judge Curtain of a seedy looking specimen who was brought before him for petty larceny the other day.

"Yes, yer honor," was the answer.

"Then how is it that you are here?"

"Dunno, yer honor," grinned the thief.

Nor did any one else seem to know.

This time the judge gave him two years, but six months later I saw him walking calmly down the Bowery one night.

That's the way it goes in New York and always has.

If you are ever going to make a successful detective you have got to mind your own business strictly and not attempt to correct the morals of those over you. Nothing but trouble for yourself can ever result.

FOOTNOTE:

[1] It is to illustrate Sam Kean's shrewdness at this particular point that I cite the case, to show how easily we may be thrown off the scent when the criminal suspects.—O. K. B.

CHAPTER IV
DISGUISES

My chapter on shadowing was such a long one, that I am afraid I have tired my reader out.

Still, shadowing is a very important feature of the detective business, and must receive particular attention if you want to be a success.

Let us now discuss disguises, the most important thing of all, perhaps.

There is far less disguising done by detectives than most people imagine.

It requires an artist to make a success in this line.

I flatter myself that I have been exceedingly successful as a disguiser, and at one time in my life my great forte was disguising as an old woman. I sometimes do that yet, but not very often, for it is a terribly dangerous part to play.

Now I can't be expected to expose my secret methods of changing my appearance which it has taken me a life time to learn.

Nor can any other detective. They simply won't do it. I'll advise, but further than that I cannot go.

A poorly arranged disguise is worse than none at all, for a sharp criminal can almost always penetrate it, and the moment he does it's all up with you, of course.

For ordinary work full disguises are not necessary.

But a detective should keep a smooth-shaven face and closely-cropped hair at all times, so that by slipping on a false mustache or a wig he can alter his whole appearance. This is about as far as it usually is necessary to go.

Suppose my man who went with the defaulter to South America had depended on a disguise how far do you suppose he could have got without being discovered?

You see the point. A calm exterior at all times and unbounded assurance is better than the best disguise.

Of course if a man is a bit of a ventriloquist it is a great help, but this is a rare gift, and not always to be depended upon even with those who possess it.

Change of clothing will do much. I always carry several hats; they are made expressly for me, and can be stowed away on my person. My usual coat is reversible; so is my vest, but with the trousers you can do nothing in a hurry, of course.

A stand-up collar in place of a turn-down, a colored necktie instead of a black one, a few skillfully-placed lines about the eyes and mouth will change your whole appearance more than you have any idea.

This is about all I've got to say on the subject of disguises. It is something every man must learn for himself. The best detectives rarely employ them, but they are sometimes an absolute necessity for all that.

Dave Doyle, at the very beginning of his career, began to show marked ability in making up a disguise.

I remember one case in particular where I sent him after some green goods men in which he did very clever work in that line. Let him tell the story himself.

Dave Doyle and the Green Goods Men

When Old King Brady gave me that circular of the green goods men, sent to him from Bean Corners, Kentucky, by an honest store-keeper, and told me that he expected I would bag the fellows, I own up I was kind of stumped.

"You've got to get good evidence against them, Dave," he said. "It won't be no use for you to pull 'em in without you can prove just what they are."

The first thing I did was to ask Old King Brady to give me instructions, but he wouldn't do nothing of the sort.

"Work it your own way," he said. "I won't promise that I shan't put another man on either. I want to see how you make out."

Well, the first thing I did was to take a long walk up Broadway and think. I can always think better on Broadway than anywhere else.

I had read the circular over two or three times and about knew it by heart.

It was signed by a feller named Clancy and stated, as all them green-goods circulars do, that he had some of the best counterfeit money in the world—so good that no one could ever detect it—which he was willing to sell at such a cheap price that a man could easy get rich in a week or two if he could only work the stuff off.

Of course there was no address. The fellow what got the circular was told to write to the New York post-office and make an appointment at some hotel.

This is just what I done. I wrote a letter to Mr. Clancy and sent it out to a cousin of mine in Wisconsin to mail. I didn't tell any one I done this.

After about ten days I got a letter from my cousin enclosing one from Mr. Clancy.

He was very glad that I had sense enough to take in the greatest opportunity of the age. He would meet me at Van Dyke's hotel in the Bowery, just as I said, and would soon show me the way to get rich.

I said in my answer that I'd be in front of the hotel on a certain day at a certain hour, and would blow my nose twice with a red handkerchief. He was to know me by that. The name I gave was Spalding. I made out I kept a country store at Jim's River—that's the name of the town where my cousin lived.

Of course I was on hand at the appointed time.

So was Mr. Clancy.

I was made up just a little—not much—but I wasn't made up like Mr. Spalding.

Not a bit of it. I got Sam Kean to do that, for I had told him all about the case, and asked him to help me out, which of course he did, for ever since that night I saved his life in that Broadway store, Sam and me has been the best of friends.

Sam stood right in front of the Van Dyke just as the big clock behind the bar was striking three.

I was just across Bayard street, standing in the doorway of the New England, taking the whole business in.

No sooner had Sam pulled out his red handkerchief, and given a snort that knocked the cornet fellow in the Dime Museum across the street silly, than I saw a good-looking chap with black whiskers and very respectable, come across the Bowery.

He walked right by me, so I got a good look at him. Next thing I knew he was talking to Sam.

I watched 'em for near half an hour. He seen me watching, too, and got nervous, but this was just what I wanted, so I never budged.

Bimeby he give it up, and Sam went back into the hotel, Mr. Clancy making tracks down the Bowery as fast as ever he could go.

"That's all right," says I. "So far first-rate."

I wanted to speak to Sam most awfully, but I didn't dare, for you see I couldn't tell who might be watching, so I just scooted down the Bowery, and catching up with man, gave him a tap on the shoulder.

You'd just orter seen him turn on me, but I was as cool as a cucumber, you bet.

"What yer want?" he says.

"You," says I, showing my shield.

He turned white and then began to bluff.

"Oh, you go to blazes!" he says. "You don't know what you're talking about."

"Yes, I do," I says. "I know well enough. I'm sent after Clancy, the green goods man, and you're the very fellow, but if you'll jest keep your shirt on we may fix the thing up."

"Say, young feller," he whispered, catching my arm, "say, I ain't Clancy. Clancy's a friend of mine, but if they're onto our racket mebbe we might fix it up together for him."

"Of course, if you're only reasonable," I says.

"Oh, I'm the most reasonablest feller you ever seen," he says, "if you only rub me the right way. Let's come and have a drink. I seen you watching me back there, and I know'd you was a detective. I know'd, too, that you was one of the sensible kind."

Well, we went and had a drink—in fact we had three or four.

"Are the police onto us?" he says.

"They are," says I. "If they wasn't, why would I be here? They know all about you, and I advise you as a friend to change your quarters at once."

"To-day?" he says, looking kind of scared like.

"Yes, to-day."

"Won't to-morrow do?" he says, laying a twenty dollar bill down on the table where we was sitting.

"Green goods?" says I, picking up the bill.

"Not much," says he, laughing. "I guess you know what green goods amounts to as well as I do, Reilly,"—Reilly was the name I give him when we first began to talk.

"To-morrow won't do. I'm on the case to-day," I says, "but to-morrow I've got to go to Boston, and they may put on another man when I tell them I saw you trying to scoop in a sucker at the Van Dyke."

"But you won't tell 'em?" he says.

"Oh, I'll have to," says I. "How do I know that some other feller wasn't watching me same as I was watching you?"

He looked kind of nervous and bothered like, and I knew why.

"Look here, boss," I says, "how long do you want?"

"Only about an hour," he says eager like, "and then I'll be ready to move, and there'll be a hundred dollars dropped anywheres you say."

"It's a go," says I. "Is that sucker well lined?"

"Three thousand," says he. "I seen a thousand of it meself, and I know there's more."

I may as well mention that Old King Brady lent me a thousand to work with—real green goods; not a good bill among the lot, I thought.

"When are you going to meet him?" I says.

"About five o'clock," says he, "in front of the Astor House. He's afraid to move about in daylight for fear the police will go for him. Ha—ha! the fool. He's just about the greenest I ever seen, yet he seems to be an intelligent kind of a chap, too."

"You shall have the time," says I. "I won't report till six o'clock—will that do?"

"Oh, elegantly! Where'll you lay in the meanwhile?"

"Is there a back way out of this place?"

"You bet there is."

"Then that's enough. I'll manage the rest."

"An' the hundred dollars?"

I gave him a fictitious address to which I told him to mail the money—as though he would have done it in any case.

Then we separated, I going out the back way, he by the front.

So far my little scheme had worked to a charm.

When I got round into Chatham Square I looked in every direction for Mr. Clancy without being able to get a sight of him. At last I slid into a certain saloon just above the Atlantic Garden. I expected to find Mr. Spalding of Jim's River waiting for me there and I did.

I made for the wash-room, and presently he followed.

"What luck, Sam?" I whispered, as soon as I made sure that we were alone.

"Bully—he bit."

"I should say so. You showed him the green goods?"

"Yes: he was so struck with the bigness of the pile that he never stopped to look at them particularly—he feels dead sure they're all straight."

"You didn't find out where his place is?"

"Ah, no, I'm to meet him at the Astor House at 5, and he's to take me there."

"I know all that," I answered hurriedly. "Off with your clothes, old man."

"Not here, Dave," he says.

"Yes, here. We'll change a piece at a time. Must do it. All would be spoiled if we were to be seen together."

It was ticklish changing, but we got through with it splendid.

There was a glass in the place, and when I looked at myself I declare I could hardly believe it wasn't Sam in his disguise what was standing there, but of course Sam hadn't red hair, so he didn't look much like me.

I didn't want that, though—didn't expect it. 'Twasn't part of the game.

"Lay low now, young feller," says I, "and don't let 'em see you. If there's any sign of a row you just sail right in."

"You bet I will!" says he. "I ain't forgot, Dave, that you saved my life twice," which was all very well for him to say, and I had no objection to his thinking so, though, between ourselves, I never felt that that fellow Opdyke had the courage to shoot.

Well, I was at the Astor House at five o'clock, feeling a little bit shaky I will admit.

I seen him coming across from the post office. He'd been to get more green goods letters from country suckers, I s'pose.

First off I thought he was going past, but pretty soon he saw me and steered straight for me.

I watched him close as he gave me one sharp look. Then I knew I was safe.

"You're on time," he says, coming up close to me. "See, I've been over to the post-office, look at this bunch of letters. They are all from fellows who've tried my goods and want more. That's the kind of business I do."

"Let me read one of the letters so I'll know you ain't foolin' me," I says, doing Sam's country voice as well as I could.

I saw him come the flim-flam and snake a letter out of his pocket and work it into the bundle.

That was the letter he gave me to read, of course, and equally of course it was a blooming fake.

It told how the writer had used up ten thousand dollars in green goods in three months without ever having a complaint.

He was the slickest fellow with his hands ever I seen. He got another out of his pocket somehow, pretending to get it out of the pile, and I never seen him, although I was looking for that very thing.

"Seems to be a good business," says I.

"You bet," says he.

"Can we go now?" says I.

"We could have gone this afternoon if it hadn't been for you," says he. "There's nothing at all to fear. I've been doing this thing too long not to know how to manage the racket, you bet."

"Where's your place?" says I.

"Come with me and I'll show you," says he.

I asked him if he was sure there wasn't no one watching us, which gave me an excuse to look 'round for Sam, who had stopped over by the post office. I couldn't see nothing of him, though, and I wondered where he'd gone.

"Come on; it's all safe," says Clancy. "I've got the biggest pull with the police of any man in New York. Why, I pay the commissioners their little divvy. I don't bother with no captains even. There isn't an officer of the force what would dare to touch me."

I could hardly keep from laughing as I followed him around into Ann street, where gamblers and green goods men used to be a big sight plentier in them days than they are now.

We got to a door on the left hand side just beyond the alley.

I thought he was going up-stairs to Jack Bridge's place, but no, he made a dive down into a lager beer saloon in the basement, took me into a back room and then, unlocking a door, we landed in a little box of a place about four by five, where there was nothing but a stove, a desk and a couple of chairs.

He locked the door first of all—then he turned on me.

I tell you now if I wasn't measuring that man it's a caution!

"I wonder which of us two's got the most muscle," thinks I.

"Let's see your money, Mr. Spalding!" says he, handing me a cigar and lighting one himself.

"Let's see yours!" says I. "Gimme a light!"

"You're a cool one," says he. "D'yer 'spose I'm going to give up my green goods and take my chances of getting my pay?"

"But you've seen my money once."

"Oh, all right. You're suspicious. You think I ain't straight. That's what's the matter with you, my boy."

"Not at all. I only want to be on the safe side. I haven't come all the way from Wisconsin to be sucked in—let me tell you that."

"You needn't holler so," he says. "I hain't deef. Do you want every one in the saloon to hear you?"

"You don't think there's no danger, do you?" I says.

"No, I guess nothing serious is done yet," says he, "but to make all sure I'll just step out and look how the land lays."

I knew his game. He'd gone to make ready to shift the bags—it was the old dodge. I made up my mind to use the minute I had for all it was worth. There was two doors to the place, the one leading into the saloon we'd came in by. I wanted to see where the other led to and I found out, for I opened it with one of my skeleton keys. Theater Alley was outside.

I didn't fasten the door, and had no more'n time to get back to the desk where he'd left me than Mr. Clancy was in again.

"It's all right," he says. "Nobody tumbled. Don't talk so loud again—that's all. Now I'll show you the goods, and we'll close this little transaction in just about two seconds. I want you to understand, my friend, that this is no saw-dust swindle. I know you think so, but you are as much mistaken as though you'd lost your shirt. There'll be no sending the goods by express. No, sir. I shall give them to you right in this room, and here they are."

He opened a drawer in the desk and took out a big pile of new greenbacks—straight money, mind you, every bit of it. It takes money to run a green-goods business, I want you to understand.

"How much'll you take?" says he, after I had examined one or two sample bills till I told him I was satisfied.

"Guess I'll strike in with a thousand dollars' worth," says I. "How much'll that buy?"

"Three thousand," he says. "I'm going to be liberal with you, Spalding, and give you three for one."

"Wall," says I as though I was thinking like, "if that's the case you'd better make it two thousand."

"Say three?"

"Hain't got so much."

"But you said you had up at the Van Dyke."

"Wall, letter go," I says. "You see, three thousand in counterfeit bills was just what I had."

He counted out his money and I counted mine.

Then he counted mine and I counted his.

"How you going to carry it?" says he, kinder nervous like.

His eyes were fixed so sharp on his own money in my hands that he hardly looked at mine, and as the place was kinder dark never seemed to tumble to the fact that it wasn't all O.K.

"Carry it in my pockets," says I.

"That pile?" says he — "you see it was all ones and fives, while mine was in fifties and hundreds and there was a slew of 'em. You can't do it. You'd be overhauled before you could get to the Herald office. I'll lend you my grip sack," he says.

It was the old dodge — just what I'd been expecting. I felt kind of nervous myself then, especially for Old King Brady's counterfeit money, for it's against the law for any one to handle counterfeit money — even detectives are not excepted, I want you to understand, and my boss had told me he'd hold me responsible if it wasn't got back.

He put his money in the bag and mine in the desk.

Then he put the bag on the desk and began jumping round all of a sudden, whispering that there was a row in the saloon and he'd have to go out and see what it was. There must have been a row if noise went for anything, but I've no doubt it was a put up job.

He ran to the door, and I pretended to follow him, but all the same I had my eye peeled for the bag, and saw it disappear through a panel in the back of the desk just as I had expected, and another just like it come in its place.

"It's all right; only two fellers fighting," he says, popping in next minute. "Now, then, everything is all straight, and you'd better light out as soon as you can, for that fight may draw the cops in."

He picked up the bag and handed it to me.

"You'd better go out this way," he says, pointing to the door.

Now the ticklish time had come.

Where was Sam? It had been arranged that he should follow me and be ready to help in case I needed him, but I hadn't seen nothing of him when I looked out.

Clancy seemed surprised when he found the door unlocked.

"Slide right out," he whispered. "I hear some one coming."

"All right," says I, "but you'll come, too," and I grabbed him by the collar, and, before he knew what was coming, was dragging him up the steps.

I'd dropped the bag and had yanked out my revolver, but I never got the chance to use it—oh, no!

Quick as a wink he out with a knife and tried to get at me.

I saw the flash of the blade and managed to knock up his arm.

Then I went down right in the alley and he on top of me.

I tell you I was scared. Things began to dance before my eyes, and I thought I was a goner when all at once two men jumped out from behind a lot of ash barrels and pulled him over on his back.

"Old King Brady!" I heard him gasp, and there it ended as far as he was concerned.

"Hold him, Dave!" hollered Old King Brady, diving through the door.

Me and the other fellow held on like grim death, you bet. Let's see, I forgot to say that the other fellow was Sam.

That was about the end of it altogether, for Old King Brady scooped in his pal at the point of the revolver just as he was coming through the door to find out what the row was all about.

It was a mighty lucky thing for me, too, that they happened to come along just as they did, for if they hadn't I honestly believe I'd been a dead man in about one minute's time.

We scooped 'em both, but we didn't get their money, for of course the bag was stuffed with old newspaper. What became of it we never knew. Old King Brady found his in the drawer of the desk, though, and when I began to talk about it as counterfeit he only laughed at me.

"I was fooling you about that, Dave," he said. "It's every dollar of it good."

Note.—Of course I wouldn't have dared to handle counterfeit money any more for that purpose than any other, for it's entirely against the law even to have the stuff in your possession.

I own I let Dave believe that it was counterfeit, although I didn't actually tell him so, and I did this because I thought he'd be too cautious with it and spoil the whole game if he thought it was good.

Of course I ran the risk of losing it—I knew that. I expected to lose it, but I was willing to take the chances for the sake of accomplishing my ends.

Now I must say that my pupil displayed considerable ingenuity in handling the case, and as I had never asked him, and he had never told me any of his plans from the moment he began to work, he was justly surprised that I happened along as I did.

But it was no accident.

I knew all about it. I saw the meeting at the Van Dyke, I overheard the conversation in the saloon, I followed them from the Astor House to Ann street, and was peering through the window when the transfer of the money was made.

Dave told Sam Keen all about the business, and Sam, by my direction, told me.

I had put the boy on his mettle, but I didn't propose to see him harmed, and he came precious near losing his life as it was.

Now there's an example of how I can shadow. I'd say more about it, but I don't want to boast.

I changed my appearance three times that afternoon. Sam knew me, for he helped me, but Dave never had the slightest suspicion that he was under "Old King Brady's" eye.

We sent those two rascals up for a long term, and so far as I know, they served it out. I presume the saloon keeper got the money and kept it. Of course he was one of the gang, and I closed up his place in a hurry, but as I could prove nothing against him he was soon set free.

Dave, adopting Sam's disguise, was as skillful a piece of business as I ever did.

I don't think Clancy—that wasn't his name by the way—has the slightest idea to this day that he was not dealing with the same person from first to last.

CHAPTER V
RINGING IN

Another very important duty that a detective often has to perform is to "ring in with the gang."

To arrest a criminal without having first obtained sufficient evidence to convict him of his crimes, seldom leads to any good result.

Often gangs of thieves organize for business, and if you get one you get all of them, as a rule, for thieves seldom have any honor among themselves, the old saying to the contrary, nevertheless.

Now to catch a gang like this it is often necessary to select a man to join them, a very ticklish business, by the way.

If the thieves are young men, you've got to get a young man to do the job. I'd be no use at all in such a case.

I remember shortly after the green goods case that an order came to me from the inspector to look into the matter of a gang of young toughs who were believed to make their headquarters in an unused sewer away up on First avenue.

For a long time these scoundrels had maintained a perfect reign of terror in the neighborhood of East 66th street, knocking men down and robbing them in broad daylight, breaking into stores, coming the flim-flam game on women, and all that sort of business.

There's just such a gang operating on the West side of New York now, and the police seem quite powerless to do anything to put them down.

When the matter was placed in my hands I sent for Dave and told him that he must join that gang, find out their secret hiding-place and then betray them into my hands.

Dave heaved a sigh.

"Couldn't you get somebody else to do that beside me, Mr. Brady?" he asked.

"Why, Dave," said I, "you have been selected because I think you just the man for the job. What's the matter with you going? Why do you object?"

"Well, to tell the trute, Mr. Brady (Dave always dropped into his old New York accent the moment he was the least excited), that gang is a tough one."

"You are afraid?"

"Oh, no!"

"I could hardly believe it after all the evidence I have had of your courage. What, then?"

"Bad luck to it all, me first cousin, Patsey Malloy, is running that gang," he blurted out. "You wouldn't have me go against my own flesh and blood!"

"Now you look here, young man," said I, going up to him and shaking my finger in his face. "You just want to understand one thing, and that is, if you are ever going to make a successful detective, you've got to lay all personal considerations aside. This Patsey Malloy—is he a bad one?"

"You're right, he is!" replied Dave gloomily.

"Has he broken the law?"

"A t'ousand times!"

"And you are under your solemn oath to arrest all lawbreakers?"

Dave looked confused.

"Can't we fix it no way so's to save Patsy?" he asked.

"If that could be done I suppose you would just as soon see the rest bagged as not?" said I.

"Why, of course!" he answered, hastily. "And I think it can be fixed. I'll see Patsy and let him know it's either a question of his turning State's evidence and giving me the gang or having some one else put on what'll scoop 'em all in."

"Would he do that?" I asked.

"Why, of course, rather than be took himself," replied Dave, looking surprised that I should ask such a question.

That settled it so far as Dave was concerned. I told him that I'd think about it and let him know. I saw at once that he was not the man for the work. Then I sent for Sam Kean.

As soon as he came I told him the whole story.

"Do you think you could ring in with that gang?" I asked.

"I'd like to try ever so much," he said. "I've wanted this long time to see what I could do with the roughest classes."

"Ain't you afraid?"

"Not a bit of it."

"If they get an idea of the truth they'll certainly kill you. Your life wouldn't be worth two cents."

"I'll take the risk, Mr. Brady," he said, boldly.

"All right," said I; "you shall do it; but you must work quick. I want you to begin to-night."

"I'll do it, sir," he said, and he did do it most effectually. Let him tell the rest of the story himself.

Joining the Gang

It was a cold night when I joined the sewer gang.

Old King Brady says I must make a short story of it, so I'll just begin in the middle and not tell how I located the gang—how I found that one of their hanging out places was a certain gin mill on the corner of First avenue and Seventy-third street; how I learned that they numbered more than seventy, ranging in age from twelve years to thirty. Briefly I found out all that and more.

It was a howling wilderness up in that neigborhood in those days, though it's all altered now; literally howling that night, for the wind blew a perfect gale, as it is very apt to do in the month of March.

I knew all about the neighborhood, for during the week I had been scouring it in every direction collecting evidence.

I heard of men being waylaid and knocked down in broad daylight, or unwary drunkards being lured into those solitudes, robbed and thrown over the rocks into the East River; of burglaries and all sorts of outrages being committed. Yes, I want you to understand that gang was tough.

So was I—in appearance.

I wore a pair of ragged trousers, old shoes with my frozen toes almost on the ground. Overcoat I had none, and the coat I did have was thin, dirty and ragged, buttoned up to the throat to conceal a fearful-looking shirt, under which were three others, or I should certainly have frozen to death. As for my hat, I need only say that I picked it out of the ash scow at the Seventeenth street dump.

When I reached the lumber shed on the corner of Sixty-ninth street I stopped and whistled, leaning up against the fence.

Presently I heard a voice speak through a knot-hole in the fence and say:

"Is it you?"

"Yes," said I.

"All O.K.?"

"Yes," said I. "I'm to meet him in ten minutes. I had a long talk with him last night and all is fixed."

"Where is it?" asked the voice.

"Couldn't find out," I replied. "You'll have to follow me and see."

"All right. Be very careful," said the voice—then all was quiet.

I had worked hard to get as far as I had got in the business. How I managed to get acquainted with one of the leading spirits of the gang I ain't going to tell.

It is enough to say that I had got acquainted with him and that he had promised to initiate me that night.

"Red McCann"—that was his name. I met him in the gin-mill ten minutes later.

He and two other toughs were waiting for me by appointment. They greeted me in the most friendly manner and we had several beers at my expense.

It was a great night for me, and I was expected to treat. I was going to "join the gang."

Soon we started across lots working down toward the river. Just what street we were near at last I can't say, for but few were opened then, and these being cut through the solid rock all looked alike. It was terrible cold, and I want you to understand that I was glad to get to the end of the journey at last.

"Ain't we most there?" I asked of Red McCann. "I'm just about perished."

"Oh, you'll be there soon enough, cully," he answered, winking at his companion, a fellow called "Schnitz." Whether it was really his name or not, I'm sure I don't know.

I saw the wink, and for the first time I began to wonder whether, after all, I had not deceived myself in thinking that I had deceived these fellows as to my true character.

But, no; I couldn't believe it—I wouldn't believe it.

I had worked so hard to accomplish my purpose. I had gone to lengths that made me shudder to think of.

Beside, I knew if they even suspected me my life was scarce worth a rush. I forced myself—absolutely forced myself—not to be afraid.

"Is it much further, Red?" I asked in my best "tough" dialect.

"Only a little way," he answered. "Do you see that house right by the river bank?"

"Yes."

"Do you see de woods on de left?"

"The woods," was a little clump of locust trees, once a shady grove in some gentleman's grounds in the days when the house would have been called a mansion.

"I see," I said.

"Well, we get into the sewer through that house by way of de cellar," answered Red. "We've got a underground passage cut jist like you read about in dime novels. Oh, I tell you it's bully! We've got feather beds and eat off chiny dishes. We only take our beer out of silver mugs——"

"You lie," broke in Schnitz laughing; "we keep our beer in silver kegs and drink it outer gold steins."

"You're fooling me, boys," said I, in dismay, an icy coldness striking around my heart.

"Not much, you son of a gun!" cried Red. "It's you who are trying to fool us. Hey fellers! Here we are! Let's initiate Detective Kean!"

Can you fancy my feelings at that moment?

If you can't try and fancy them at the next, when I suddenly found myself surrounded by twenty or thirty of the toughest-looking specimens I ever laid my eyes on.

We had reached the grove now, and a man seemed to spring from behind every tree.

I saw that my midnight mission was already accomplished.

Make no mistake—I had joined the gang!

It was no use to attempt to defend myself.

They were around me like a pack of wolves in an instant, a dozen hands held me, a dozen more were going through my clothes, possessing themselves of revolvers, knives, money—everything, even to my official shield, which, like a fool, I had loose in my trousers' pocket.

If ever I felt sick it was then, but I had hope.

The voice which talked to me through the lumber yard fence was Old King Brady's.

He ought to be on hand with a posse of police even now.

"Oh, you needn't look for your friends," cried Red McCann sneeringly. "We seen you talking with them down by the lumber yard. We've fixed all that—we've given 'em the proper steer.

"Hey fellers!" he added, "this is the bloke what tought he was goin' ter ring in wid us. What'll we do wid him! It's for you to say."

"Punch him! Slug him! Shoot him! Drown him?"

These and several other pleasing suggestions were offered by the crowd.

Where was Old King Brady?

Was it as Red claimed that he had been thrown off the scent.

I felt that I was lost then, and I am willing to admit that I gave myself up to die, for they fell upon me like savages, kicking and beating me, dragging me at last to the edge of the rocky bluffs which overhung the East river, and pushing me over.

Before I knew what was coming I went whirling through the air with frightful velocity, striking the water below with a resounding splash.

That is the way I joined the gang!

Never shall I forget the moment when I rose to the surface and began struggling with that terrible current which sweeps through the narrow channel between Blackwell's Island the New York shore.

It seemed hours since I had fallen, yet it could scarce have been seconds.

Up on the hill I could hear men shouting, and as I straggled toward the rocks I saw Old King Brady and his policemen appear on the bluffs and look down.

"Help! help! help!" I shouted, but the wind swept my voice over to the island. To my despair I saw Old King Brady turn away and I knew that he had not heard.

"Help! help! Help, Mr. Brady!" called another voice right before me as if in echo of my own.

I raised my eyes and looked ahead.

I was near the rocks now, swimming as well at my bruised and frozen limbs would permit.

There, crouching upon them, I saw the figure of one of the gang whom I instantly recognized as a fellow who had been particularly active in the attack upon myself.

Oh, how my heart sank!

I turned on my back and was about to strike out into the deep channel, when suddenly I saw Old King Brady coming back to the edge of the bluff.

"Hold on, Sam. Hold on! Don't go back for God's sake!" called the fellow on the rocks in a familiar voice.

He leaned forward, caught my foot, and began dragging me in shore.

Did I resist him?

Oh, no! I guess not.

I was so surprised, so overcome, that I think I must have fainted.

When I came to myself a moment later, I was lying on the rocks above the reach of the tide, and bending over me were Old King Brady and the young tough.

"Kean! Kean! rouse yourself!" exclaimed the detective. "I was just a moment or two slow. Thank goodness! he's coming round all right again! You've been deceived, Kean; they're on to you— —"

"Well, I should think I might know it," I answered, somewhat testily. "I've been sucked in, fooled, played with—it's a wonder I wasn't killed."

"Which you might have been if it hadn't been for our friend here," he answered, glancing at the young man who had appeared upon the rocks. "It's all right though. You've tracked 'em here, and that's been the means of bringing about just what we want, or will be. This young man is going to show us the way into the sewer, he says."

"To turn informer?" said I. "Why, he's one of the gang, you know."

"Yes, yes, and here come *my* gang down the rocks at last. Now, then, young man, pilot the way, and I'll make it worth your while, you can be very sure."

He raised his lantern, which he had drawn from his pocket, and threw its light before the villain's face, starting back as he did so with an exclamation of surprise.

"Dave! Dave Doyle! It can't be," he burst out.

"But it is, though, Mr. Brady," was the quiet reply. "You wouldn't trust me, so I had to do this job myself. I've done it too. Call your men, get ready your revolvers. I'm going to show you the secret way into the sewer, and there's nothing in the world to prevent you from capturing the whole gang."

Note.—Well, I own I was surprised when my lantern suddenly revealed Dave standing there upon the rocks.

You see, I hadn't been thinking anything about the fellow, so why should I expect to see him? I was taken all aback.

I presume my readers expected an entirely different termination to this story.

Let me add, so did I.

I thought Sam was succeeding splendidly, I never dreamed that Dave had moved in the matter till I saw through his carefully arranged disguise as we three stood there on the rocks.

I have introduced this case simply to show you how detectives sometimes get left as well as other folks.

It was Dave, not Sam who showed us the secret entrance to the sewer in which the gang had their headquarters, and whither they had now retreated in fancied security. I had not been deceived by the false "steer."

But I have not space enough left to tell how we captured them.

Let it suffice to say that we did capture them, that we scooped them in completely, and during the brief fight none fought better than Dave Doyle who captured his cousin with his own hands.

To this day I doubt if Mr. Patsy Malloy knows that it was Dave.

We broke up the sewer gang forever, and sent a lot of them over to the island, and now for the point I want to bring out strong.

Every man to his own kind.

That's the best rule a detective has to follow.

If it is hard to make a silk purse out of a sow's ear, it is equally hard to make a sow's ear out of a silk purse.

I tried to make a tough out of Sam Kean, and I failed.

Why, Dave, who had secretly joined the sewer gang a week before Sam got ready to begin, told me that they saw through Sam from the very start.

"He couldn't fool 'em, Mr. Brady," he said. "I was awful sorry I couldn't warn him, and I would have done so if I'd knowed he was going to come that night, but I didn't until it was too late. I meant all along to tell him in time."

"Why couldn't he fool 'em, Dave?" I asked.

"Can't you tell a tough when you see one?"

"I rather think I can."

"Then so can we tell a gentleman. I'm a tough myself, and I know."

He was right, but be overstated the case in calling himself a tough.

Dave Doyle had been born among them and brought up among them, but he never was a tough himself, but a thoroughly honest fellow from the word go.

When I intimated that he was not the man for the sewer-gang job, on account of his relationship with the leader, he resolved to show me that he was the man, and he did.

Dave succeeded without an effort where Sam, with all his efforts, failed, and came within an ace of losing his life.

Therefore, I say, every one to his place.

But Sam Kean made a splendid detective. I used him as my society man for years, until he went off at last on his own hook.

So also with Dave. He remained my man for the work in the slums and a better one I never had.

Now then, boys, has all this taught you how to become a detective?

I'm afraid not.

I'm afraid that after all you feel disappointed that I have not laid down some cast-iron rule which will throw you into the high tide of success in our business like the touch of Aladdin's lamp.

Let me say to the disappointed ones confidentially give up the idea of ever becoming a detective.

It will be just as well, in fact, a great deal better.

If you can't see the force of all my remarks, if you can't learn the lessons contained in the cases cited, believe the old man when he tells that your genius runs in other channels, and you will do better to leave the detective business severely alone.

As for the rest of you—you who have read this little book and enjoyed it, I mean—there is at least reason to believe that you might make successful detectives if you have a mind to persevere.

But is the game worth the candle?

Think what a detective's life means.

Hard work, exposed to cold, hunger, thirst, great danger, and every privation. I've been through all of these things, and just so sure as you embark in the business you'll find yourselves there too.

Another thing which I haven't mentioned that shouldn't be forgotten. It is the social position which the detective occupies—always has and always will.

By nine men out of ten he is looked upon as a spy, and regarded with dislike and distrust.

A detective can have but few friends; many have none.

Men may flatter him and praise his shrewdness, but they will ever shun him and keep him at arm's length.

I have grown rich at the business—very rich—but let me say right here that I am one in a thousand.

Most of our detectives work hard and suffer much, and in the end die poor and despised.

If you don't believe me hunt up some detective and ask him; he'll tell you the same thing.

Still if you must be a detective start right and be honest, and you will always be able to respect yourself, no matter what others may think.